KINGSTEIGNTON

of Yesteryear

Richard Harris

OBELISK PUBLICATIONS

ALSO BY THE AUTHOR
Kingsteignton Collection
Other Titles in This Series
Ashburton of Yesteryear, *John Germon & Pete Webb*
Brixham of Yesteryear, Parts I, II and III, *Chips Barber*
Teign Valley of Yesteryear, *Chips Barber*
Princetown of Yesteryear Parts I and II, *Chips Barber*
Pinhoe of Yesteryear, *Chips Barber*

We have over 120 Devon titles, for further details of these or any of our titles, please send a first class stamp to Obelisk Publications at the address below, or telephone (01392) 468556

"To Dad"

Acknowledgments
I should like to thank Mrs E. Auton, Mr W. Bartlett, Mrs S. Carter, Mrs A. Chammings, Mrs M. Davis, Mrs J. Ewers, Mr K. Gibbs, Mr F. Hamlyn, Mr E. Hewings, Miss B. Lawes, Mrs S. Morris, Mrs M. Nicks, Mrs K. Partridge, Mr S. Sanders, Mrs V. Sharp, Mr L. Sweetland, Mr M. Thorne,Mr B. Tothill, Mrs D. Vallance, Mrs L. White and Mrs M. Wildash for their kind loan of photographs and also Mr N. Toyne (photographer) for permission to use the pictures on shown on pages 9 (bottom) and 10 (top).

First published in 1996 by
Obelisk Publications, 2 Church Hill, Pinhoe, Exeter, Devon
Designed by Chips and Sally Barber
Typeset by Sally Barber
Printed in Great Britain by The Devonshire Press Limited, Torquay, Devon

KINGSTEIGNTON

of Yesteryear

We'll start this nostalgic tour through a 'Kingsteignton of Yesteryear' in the centre of the village where we have an unusual view of the Fountain, the function of which was to provide a watering place for passing animals. Taken on a wet day in the mid 1920s, there is an omnibus coming from the direction of Newton Abbot, overtaking a horse and trap and a flock of sheep.

The picture below was taken about a decade later when the village butcher, Joe Honywill, could be contacted by dialling 'Newton Abbot 52' – the multi-digit telephone number was still a long way off!

This postcard was posted from the village in 1912, showing a view of the lower end of Fore Street. Kingsteignton Post Office is clearly recognisable but since then it has developed to include the adjacent premises. In the lower right hand corner the observant eye might just be able to pick out the former cycle

shop of Mr W. Pickett which was replaced, in later years, by Honywill's butcher shop shown overleaf.

When the bottom picture was taken, in the late 1920s, Fore Street was a bustling shopping centre, reflecting a more self-contained way of village life. Kelly's Directory for 1926 lists sixteen traders between the Fountain and the beginning of Vicarage Hill: two bakers, three grocers, two butchers, a tailor, a shoemaker, one dairy, one cycle agent, a hardware store, a sweetshop, the post office and two public houses.

Above can be seen the Meet of the local hunt outside the Bell Inn. The picture was taken about 1920 when this public house possessed a thatched roof. Across the road one can see the now demolished cottages of Mill Triangle, fondly remembered as "The Drang" by older inhabitants of the village. The cottage that fronted onto Crossley Moor Road was, rather humorously, called Water View, on account of the narrow strip of the leat which it overlooked.

The cottages in this second view were condemned and demolished as part of a slum clearance scheme in 1935. They stood in Berry Lane and formed a most distinctive scene with their individual miniature bridges spanning the leat. The watercourse served a multitude of uses in addition to providing a water supply. It provided power for the mills and the women of the village would often soak saltfish in it prior to cooking. It was the practice to take the portion of fish, affixed to a length of string, and tie it to one of these small bridges!

So just where is this fine bunch of upstanding Kingsteigntonians posing for the photographer? The walled garden of Berry farmhouse provides a clue and the faint-worded pub sign of the Dew Drop Inn is a giveaway. The picture was taken about 1900 and shows us that the original inn was a converted cottage, which stood on the site of the present pub. Just a few years later, in 1903, the inn above was demolished to be replaced by the one below. The new building was brick-built, the cream coloured bricks being manufactured just along the Newton Road at Hexter and Humpherson's brickworks.

This fine building was built about 1815 in the Cottage Orné style as a vicarage for the Rev Thomas Whipham. Appropriately it was originally called Vicar's Hill and the view enjoyed here is certainly a heavenly one, from the thatched verandah, as the high rolling hills rising above the Bovey Basin can be seen from this vantage point. It has since been divided into two houses and the sweeping lawns have gone to make way for new housing and a stretch of Greenhill Way. Below is a wedding picture from 1902, taken at the old vicarage. The marriage was between a local girl named Rapson and a Cornishman and shows off the incredible hat-making skills of the Edwardian milliners!

The top two pictures are of the same event, which was staged beside the Teignmouth road at Ware Barton in 1951. The top scene records the swan-song of the age of the carthorse. All around the arena are motor cars, a more potent form of horsepower whose demands were to transform the topography of the adjacent area in later years when the massive workings of the Kingsteignton by-pass carved through the adjoining fields. In the second scene people-power is being put to the test as the Watts, Blake and Bearne tug-of-war team were notching up yet another victory in an afternoon of strenuous activity.

Below an inquisitive crowd has gathered at the foot of Ware Hill in 1912 at the scene of an accident when a traction engine crashed through the hedge. You may have to look closely to see the unfortunate vehicle as it's covered in people!

Coombesend has long been a favourite route for an afternoon stroll for generations of villagers. Many people will remember the old woods of Colladown, on the left hand side of the picture, which were thickly carpeted in bluebells in spring time. Unfortunately for economic reasons this beautiful deciduous woodland was felled to be replaced by conifers in the 1950s. The poetry-inspiring view below is a familiar one for all those who travel the road to Teignmouth. It's easy to appreciate why Keats wrote these lines when he stayed in the resort in 1818:

Here all the summer could I stay,   *Where close by the stream you may have*
For there's Bishop's teign and King's teign,   *your cream,*
And Coomb at the clear teignhead,   *All spread upon barleybread.*

This picture of the Passage House, above, was taken about 1959 just after the pub had been renovated. To the left is the old skittle alley, later converted into a restaurant. The increased popularity of this riverside spot has led to much more development in more recent years.

Below is a picture postcard of the interior of Kingsteignton Church, a building which was extensively restored in 1865. The high box pews were removed, the roof was replaced and seven windows were restored. However the church retains examples of work from earlier centuries, fine examples of this being the richly decorated pillars and the octagonal font.

The church tower was built in the late 15th century with money raised by sponsorship of the wool trade. It is tapered in three stages and measures some 82 feet in height making it quite a landmark – it can be seen from miles around. The walls of the tower are some six feet thick. The Lychgate is unusual in that it possesses an arch filled with tracery, more typically found in the central arches of rood screens.

Here we have two cards of Brookside, Kingsteignton. The Fairwater Leat is also shown in both views. A lack of written records has made it difficult to establish an exact date for when this watercourse was built. If word of mouth details are to be believed it was cut by monks from Salisbury cathedral in the Middle Ages. In 1985 an archaeological dig, in Berry Meadow, found evidence that it was flanked by a 13th or 14th century ditch on the side of the meadow where the present wall is located. This lends some substance to the spoken theory passed down through the years. The message, scribbled on the back of the card below, which was posted to Plymouth in 1917, simply said "Having a lovely time on the farm." That farm was Rydon, then an isolated building some half a mile from the village, another reminder of just how much Kingsteignton has grown in size.

The above picture was taken in Crossley Moor Road in 1962. New bungalows had recently been built in the former allotment field but the winding lane had still to be realigned to accommodate its ever increasing traffic flow. The elm trees, on the left of the picture, fronted an old stable block which had a cobbled forecourt. Within a few years of this picture they were to disappear and, in turn, be replaced by more bungalows. The road follows the course of the Fairwater Stream, almost in parallel fashion and for this reason was referred to as Fairwater Lane.

A tale of two Golvers Hill views! The one above is the more recent, taken about 1955, whereas the one below was taken in the 1920s. To the right of the top picture is the thatched "Gildon's Cottage", a grade II listed building that takes its name from the Gilldene family who were settled in the parish during the 15th century. When the bottom picture was taken the bungalows in the view were regarded as 'state of the art' in terms of modern housing. The builders of the day would look to sources for materials as close to the site as possible and to this end a sand pit was excavated from a pit on the opposite side of the road. The bottom picture carried a spelling mistake that may be explained by the recorder having to write the caption in reverse on the glass plate negative – or he may have thought that 'Glovers' was more likely than 'Golvers'!

The top picture helps to show how Kingsteignton has spread into the surrounding countryside. It shows the Old Rydon Inn as viewed from Well Close (now the site of Rydon School's playing field) in 1978. In its original rural setting it's easier to appreciate the origin of its name as an isolated farm where rye was grown. The middle picture was taken in 1980, after the narrow lane had been widened to create better access for the large scale housing development that was to follow. The bottom picture dates back to 1925 when Mr Proft was mine host at the King's Arms Hotel.

Kingsteignton of Yesteryear

Kingsteignton's traffic is a bit different today! Here we have a view from the 1920s that shows Oakford, the King's Arms and the Liberal Club (now the Oakford Club). The Liberal Club's foundation stone was laid in October 1908 by Mr C. R. Buxton, a man who had been involved in a controversial incident

when, earlier that same year, there had been a lot of trouble following the declaration of results of the parliamentary by-election. Mr Buxton had been defeated by Captain Morrison-Bell by a margin of some 559 votes and the winning Conservatives quickly organised a torchlight victory procession through the Liberal heartland of Kingsteignton. Rubbing salt into the wound like this was too much for many of Kingsteignton's Liberal supporters. They strutted down Newton Road to greet the procession and fighting soon broke out, hand to hand combat being continued along the route into both Gestridge and Chudleigh Road. An elderly villager, and participant, once said "By the time we got to Turnpike (Newcross) we had all their torches and then we chased them back to Newton along the old way."

Below is a meet of the Haldon harriers at Oakford House in about 1935. The pack was first formed, in 1759, by the Rev Kitson of Shiphay, Torquay. The pack moved to Kingsteignton in the late 19th century and was kennelled at Oakford Lawn.

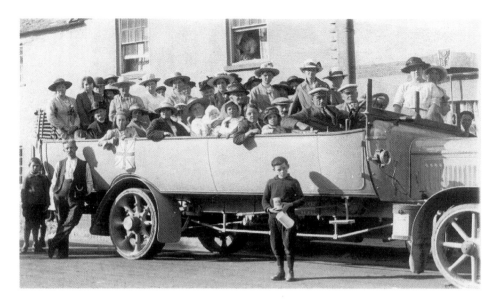

The Oakford connection continues with the above 1920s picture, which shows the merry throng of day-trippers ready to leave Oakford. The cottages behind the vehicle are now the premises of Redmayne & Co whilst those to the left of the picture were demolished in 1965 as part of a road-widening scheme.

Below is the shop window of Mr Bartlett, as it appeared in 1939, who traded from premises in Gestridge Road. Apparently you could paint a bicycle for a shilling and a table for not much more. Those were the days!

On this page we have two views of Gestridge from yesteryear. The top picture, taken about 1912, shows Yeoman's Terrace. What is now 10, Gestridge Road was once the residence of the village policeman and can be identified as the one with the Devon Constabulary plaque above the door. The picture at the bottom of the page was taken about 1900. Soon after this picture was taken the cottages on the right were demolished to be replaced by new stone-built houses by local builder, Mr A. P. Yeoman who used local stone from Rydon Quarry.

On the opposite page is a trio of pictures where the workers relied heavily on horses for their livelihoods. The top picture was taken at Moorsend Farm about 1905 when the

Sweetlands were tenants of the Clifford Estate and Chudleigh Road was bordered by open farmland. The stable block, behind Mrs Anna Sweetland, her sons, Tom and John, her husband, also Tom, still exists although in a different guise. Today it has become numbers 2 & 4 Moorsend, with its rendered walls masking all clues to its original function. The site of the former farmhouse is now covered by a bungalow development. The lower left picture shows young Ern Hewings, who spent much of his spare time assisting farmers by tending their horses. The picture beside it shows Ken Gibbs assisting Mr R. Brown on his round. The picture, which shows part of the horse and cart, was taken in 1933 and shows the gable end of Moorsend Farm.

The new building in the picture above is the Hawthorns in York Terrace. Mr Howe and his two sons were responsible for building over 200 houses in the village, ranging from terraces in Ley Lane to detached dwellings such as Longfield House in Humber Lane. Here the skilled workforce, who also built the choir stalls in the United Reformed Church, are seen posing for the photographer. Below is a charabanc outing about to depart from Ley Lane in about 1921. The butchers' shop in the background, which was Messrs Wearne and Sinclair, is now The King's Fry.

The top picture was taken looking along Exeter Road in 1934, a short time after Mr W. Whitear had converted numbers 57 & 59 into a new grocery shop. In later years it was taken over by The Newton Abbot Co-operative Society who further extended the premises to take in number 61. Note the cigarette vending machine and a solitary Austin 7. There is even less 'traffic' in the middle picture, which was taken farther along the same road. The houses along this stretch of road, including Exeter Road Garage, were

built by Mr R. Davey who was also the first proprietor of the garage.

Shown here is the little shop opposite Exeter Road Post Office. It was originally opened as a shoe repair business by Percy Earl. The shop was acquired by the young Margaret Pickett in 1932 and converted into a newsagent's. The lady outside is shop assistant Betty Passmore posing for this 1935 picture.

Before the construction of the Kingsteignton By-pass the main route to the resorts of Torbay was through the village, along Exeter Road. In the summer many residents would hang out 'Bed & Breakfast' signs to

try to catch the passing trade. The person who sent this card stayed at 152, Exeter Road in 1955. Note the cream teas being offered by Mrs Keil at the post office.

The picture below is much older and dates back to 1908 when the cavalry were still very much a part of the army. This picture was taken at the Yeomanry camp at Lambparks. The roof of Abrook Farm can just be spotted at the top of the picture.

The top picture opposite shows the sorry sight of Eagle Farm as it looked in 1980, a short time before the buildings were demolished to make way for a new housing development. However its name lives on in the street name 'Eagle Close'.

The middle and bottom pictures show the river Teign – the middle part of our village's name and part of all our lives. The middle picture of Teign Bridge was taken in 1950 before the river was realigned to make way for the extensive excavations for ball-clay which were to follow in later years. The current bridge was built in 1815 and during the removal of the old bridge the remains of three others were found underneath its foundations. It is thought that the earliest dates back to Roman times.

The clay industry has been the lifeblood of Kingsteignton and it has given employment to several generations of villagers. Above we have a young George Sanders photographed in Chudleigh Road in the early 1920s. Driving a clay cart was one of the occupations available to boys on leaving school at the turn of the century, that is from the 19th to the 20th. Within a few years they might progress to working in one of the many pits or mines in the parish. The horses that pulled these carts had a tough life hauling the carts from the floors of the quarries. In wet weather the task was even harder for the quarry floors became quagmires. Horses were not put to such arduous tasks until they were about eight or nine years old. The upright picture shows an underground working where some of the most prized clays are found. Adit mining techniques are used to obtain these clays from depths of up to 850 feet. Mr N. Vallance can be seen here working in a shaft of 'Light Blue' clay wearing the traditional miners' garments of fustians and yorks. Fustians are a type of trousers made from coarse cotton twill such as 'moleskin' which the miners found to be particularly comfortable for working in whilst 'yorks' is a dialect word for the leather straps affixed around the calves.

The years of brick and pipe making came to an end in 1968 when the old brickworks, built in the late 1880s in Newton Road, by Messrs Hexter and Humpherson, were demolished. The 165 foot high chimney was scheduled for demolition at 11.30 a.m. on 10 October but stubbornly refused to budge so work was postponed until the following day. The next morning, soon after drilling recommenced, cracks began to appear at the base of the chimney; within a few minutes it groaned and 600 tons of bricks crashed to the ground as one of the area's best-known landmarks vanished from the skyline.

The picture below shows the children of the Church School, with their

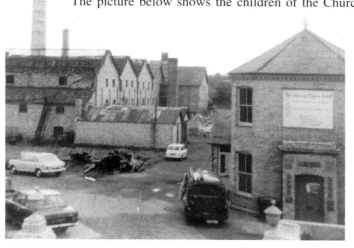

teacher Miss Butland, in 1929 when education was determined more along the lines of a religious influence. The managers of the Church School had rejected a proposal, seven years earlier, to amalgamate with the Council School. They stated their objection to any reorganisation, which was not based on the grounds of religious instruction. The pupils shown are: Back: J. Luscombe, W. Bowden, K. Veale, E. Lear, W. Vallance, B. Irwin, K. Gibbs, Miss Butland. Second row: L. Mortimore, W. Murrin, M. Walters, H. Jordan, S. Garrett, R. Frost, F. Vallance, S. Bastow, T. Murrin, G. Willcocks. Third row: D. Denley, A. Dyson, B. Farleigh, E. Cook, P. Brimmecombe, M. Priest, B. Bickham, J. Wright, J. Aggett, D. Hoare, W. Sutton. Front: J. Greenhill, J. Glanfield, G. Lofthouse, D. Germon.

In 1919 Mr W. Pearce took over as Headmaster of the Council School in Sandpath Road having served with distinction as a stretcher bearer with the Devonshire Regiment. One of the many wounded servicemen that he rescued was a certain Mr Hugh Hosegood, who was to follow him to Kingsteignton, in 1935, to take up the post of Headmaster of the new Senior School. Mr Pearce is pictured here with a class of 1939. Back row: W. Pearce, E. Farleigh, D. Clark, B. Sharp, D. Hawkins, B. Hall, K. Kelly, E. Stephens, M. Cornall, R. Finch, F. Yeo. Middle row: Y. Murrin, S. Lark, E. Hocking, J. Brimmecombe, J. Archer, B. Perryman, J. Widdecombe, P. Vickery, H. Underhay, D. Rendle. Front row: P. Germon, B. Veale, R. Hambly, S. Sanders, R. Selley, B. Tothill, I. Cann, R. Harris. The faded picture below features the Ram Roast, an event that has been traditionally held at Whitsuntide although nobody seems to know how or when it began. One explanation states that it began in the reign of Henry II when the heiress of Whiteway married the son of De la Torre. However the most likely explanation is that once there was a severe drought and on the advice of a wise woman a ram lamb was sacrificed in the dried up bed of the Fairwater Stream as an offering to the god of the spring. This had the desired effect and the water began to flow again and has done ever since.

Maypole dancing has long associations with the Ram Fair and at one time this took place in the streets. The above photo is possibly the oldest that exists of the Fair and shows the Maypole and the dancers at Oakford outside what has now become the Smugglers' fish and chip bar. The Gibson Girl costume, of the girl on the right, and the style of the children's bonnets, date the picture at about 1895. The middle picture shows the

Maypole dancers of 1934 when the children of the Council School (formerly the Chapel School) were allowed to take part for the first time. Previously it had been the sole preserve of the children from the Church School. For many years the young girls of the village have cherished the honour of being chosen as the May Queen or one of her attendants. Dressed in their finery and ready for their big day, in 1936, are P. Tooze and B. Chammings. It has, so far, proved impossible to name the third girl.

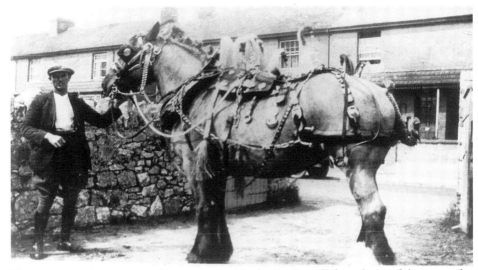

There were various competitions associated with the Ram Fair and one of them was for carthorses. Above is Mr W. Cole standing in the yard of Moorsend Farm with his winning entry in 1931. Below is Jack Edwards with his son, Basil, with their entry in the local traders' class at the Ram Fair in 1935. Their milk cart was made at the Vicarage Hill workshop of Mr W. Vallance and is a splendid example of craftsmanship of a bygone age.

Kingsteignton's footballers have enjoyed success on a number of occasions. The top picture opposite is the team from the 1937/38 season who defeated Tiverton Town 2-1 at Exeter's St James Park to lift the Geary Cup. The victorious team are shown with the committee members at Garage Lawn (where St Michael's Road now stands). Those present were – Back row: W. Eales, S. Cornall, W. Carpenter, R. Chammings, F. Veale and J. White. Middle row: J. Quantick, W. Kelly, C. Scott, J. Endacott, D. Regan, D.

Hewitt, H. Osborne, L. Johns and J. Webber. Front row: C. Hyatt, W. Cheeseworth, W. Cassels, W. Jordan, E. Howard, T. McGovern, and V. Randall. Kingsteignton's rugby team have also had their moments of glory. The picture below is from the 1922/23 season when the Cherry and Whites completed the first of what turned out to be a hat-trick of wins in the Devon Junior Cup. The winning line-up and committee members are pictured here. Back row: Ellis, E. Eddolls, Holman, T. Ponsford, J. Whiteway-Wilkinson, R. Payne, A. Discombe, Carnell, J. Bovey, W. Whiteway-Wilkinson, W. Mann, Herd. Middle row: Ponsford, T. Daw, W. Harvey, W. Field, F. Hambly, Chammings, W. Sanders. Front row: L. Knapman, T. Lock.

The competition for the Ram Fair shield used to attract entries from numerous schools in the South Devon area. The victorious Kingsteignton Church School relay team, from about 1933, are shown here. The four boys are K. Willcocks, F. Edwards, B. Edwards and D. Cordell. Their master was Mr Rabley. The orchard behind them and the corrugated fence now forms part of the St Michael's Primary School site. Below are the tough-looking and successful Watts, Blake and Bearne tug of war team as pictured at the Bell Inn in 1950. The team members were – Back row: J. Harris, N. Vallance, S. Ley, B. Bailey, W. Hannaford, R. Cousins. Front row: D. Carnell, G. Trewin, E. Parker, J. Watts, W. Strong, and J. Woodward.

Many older residents (and some not so old!) can remember the Devon General garage in Newton Road. The route from the Fountain to Newton Abbot was so profitable that it was nicknamed "The Golden Mile". In 1933 the company caused an uproar when it increased the fare from Ley Lane to Pottery Cottages from one penny to a penny ha'penny, an increase of 50 per cent. The Parochial Committee sent a letter of protest to Devon General but it was to no avail. Below are the Special Constables from the Second World War who stepped into the breach when men went off to fight. Here they are shown gathered together at the Congregational Hall in 1941. Included in their ranks are – Back row: D. Crowley, S. Daw, H. Pope, G. Partridge, G. Mason, W. Whitear. Front row: H. Mullins, A. Lear, D. McGregor, E. Good, A. Revell, S. Morris and P. C. Prior.

Throughout the war, manufacturing sites, such as Hexter and Humpherson's brickworks, were always vulnerable to attack by enemy aircraft. On one occasion an
incendiary bomb, which had been jettisoned by a bomber making its way back from an
attack on Plymouth, fell through the roof and burned its way through one of the upper
floors before landing in a kiln. Fortunately no great damage was done. The works' fire
crew is shown here, with their bowser, in 1944. From left to right they are: F. Warren,
W. Powlesland, V. Pope, C. Sharp, G. Groves, A. Gribbon, A. Baker, F. Sleeman, C.
Warren, E. Westcott, C. Brimmecombe, E. Bearne and A. Westcott.

We finish this book with a picture of the VE Day celebrations at the Recreation Ground
(now Clifford Park) on 8 May 1945. Private Jim Bray is shown cutting the cake, an
honour that he enjoyed as he was on a spell of home leave.